AF428231

WHAT'S THE MISSING LETTER?

Basic Vocabulary for Kids Picture Book

Children's Reading and Writing Books

LET'S FIND THE MISSING LETTER IN EACH WORD. GOOD LUCK!

Look at each picture and fill in the
missing letters for each word.

__nt

ap_le

HERE'S HELP!

a p

Look at each picture and fill in the missing letters for each word.

ba_y

ba_l

HERE'S HELP!

b l

Look at each picture and fill in the missing letters for each word.

ba_

b_e

HERE'S HELP!

e g

Look at each picture and fill in the missing letters for each word.

b_rd

bo_t

HERE'S HELP!

a i

Look at each picture and fill in the missing letters for each word.

bo_k

bo__

HERE'S HELP!

x   o

Look at each picture and fill in the missing letters for each word.

c_t

ca_

HERE'S HELP!

a n

Look at each picture and fill in the missing letters for each word.

_ar

c__rrot

HERE'S HELP!

a   c

Look at each picture and fill in the missing letters for each word.

cha_r

che__se

HERE'S HELP!

i e

Look at each picture and fill in the missing letters for each word.

c_in

_og

HERE'S HELP!

d o

Look at each picture and fill in the missing letters for each word.

do_l

do_r

HERE'S HELP!

o l

Look at each picture and fill in the missing letters for each word.

dr_m

du_k

HERE'S HELP!

u   c

Look at each picture and fill in the missing letters for each word.

_gg

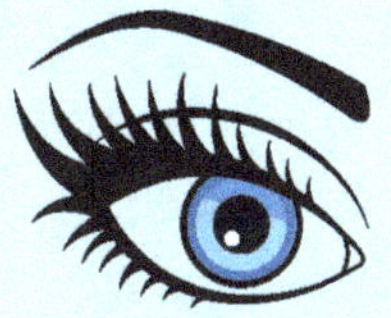

e__es

HERE'S HELP!

y e

Look at each picture and fill in the missing letters for each word.

egg_lant

el__phant

HERE'S HELP!

e   p

f_re

fi_h

HERE'S HELP!

Look at each picture and fill in the missing letters for each word.

_ood

fr_its

HERE'S HELP!

u f

Look at each picture and fill in the
missing letters for each word.

ga_e

g__ass

HERE'S HELP!

I t

Look at each picture and fill in the
missing letters for each word.

go_t

gra__es

HERE'S HELP!

a p

Look at each picture and fill in the missing letters for each word.

__at

h_use

HERE'S HELP!

h   o

Look at each picture and fill in the missing letters for each word.

ha_mer

__ce

HERE'S HELP!

m   i

Look at each picture and fill in the missing letters for each word.

ig_oo

ma_ks

HERE'S HELP!

s   l

Look at each picture and fill in the missing letters for each word.

m_ney

mo_th

HERE'S HELP!

u o

Look at each picture and fill in the missing letters for each word.

m_nkey

or_nge

HERE'S HELP!

a o

__wl

on_on

HERE'S HELP!

Look at each picture and fill in the missing letters for each word.

o_topus

pap_r

HERE'S HELP!

c e

Look at each picture and fill in the
missing letters for each word.

p_ncil

pa_da

HERE'S HELP!

n e

Look at each picture and fill in the missing letters for each word.

r_dio

ra_nbow

HERE'S HELP!

a p

Look at each picture and fill in the
missing letters for each word.

scho_l

s_n

HERE'S HELP!

a o

Look at each picture and fill in the missing letters for each word.

t_ble

tra_n

HERE'S HELP!

a i

ANSWER KEYS

Look at each picture and fill in the missing letters for each word.

a_nt

app_le

HERE'S HELP!

a p

Look at each picture and fill in the missing letters for each word.

ba_b_y

ba_l_l

HERE'S HELP!

b   l

Look at each picture and fill in the missing letters for each word.

bag

b_ee_

HERE'S HELP!

e g

Look at each picture and fill in the missing letters for each word.

b_ird

bo_at

HERE'S HELP!

a i

Look at each picture and fill in the
missing letters for each word.

bo<u>o</u>k

bo<u>x</u>

HERE'S HELP!

x   o

Look at each picture and fill in the
missing letters for each word.

c<u>a</u>t

ca<u>n</u>

HERE'S HELP!

a n

Look at each picture and fill in the
missing letters for each word.

<u>c</u>ar

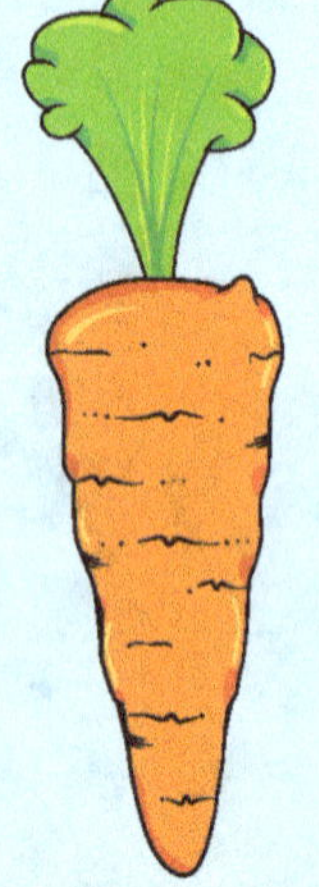

c<u>a</u>rrot

HERE'S HELP!

a   c

Look at each picture and fill in the missing letters for each word.

ch**a**ir

che**e**se

HERE'S HELP!

i e

Look at each picture and fill in the missing letters for each word.

c<u>o</u>in

<u>d</u>og

HERE'S HELP!

d o

Look at each picture and fill in the missing letters for each word.

do_l_l

do_o_r

HERE'S HELP!

o   l

Look at each picture and fill in the
missing letters for each word.

dr<u>u</u>m

du<u>c</u>k

HERE'S HELP!

u c

Look at each picture and fill in the missing letters for each word.

_**e**_gg

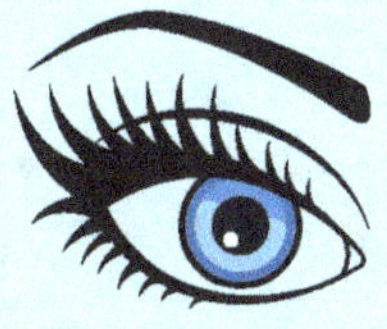

e_**y**_es

HERE'S HELP!

y   e

Look at each picture and fill in the missing letters for each word.

eggplant

elephant

HERE'S HELP!

e   p

Look at each picture and fill in the
missing letters for each word.

f<u>i</u>re

fi<u>s</u>h

HERE'S HELP!

i s

Look at each picture and fill in the missing letters for each word.

food

fr**u**i**t**s

HERE'S HELP!

u f

Look at each picture and fill in the missing letters for each word.

ga_t_e

gl_a_ss

HERE'S HELP!

l t

Look at each picture and fill in the missing letters for each word.

go_a_t

gra_p_es

HERE'S HELP!

a p

Look at each picture and fill in the
missing letters for each word.

h̲at

h̲o̲use

HERE'S HELP!

h   o

Look at each picture and fill in the missing letters for each word.

hamme<u>m</u>mer

<u>i</u>ce

HERE'S HELP!

m i

Look at each picture and fill in the missing letters for each word.

igl_oo

mas_ks

HERE'S HELP!

s   l

Look at each picture and fill in the missing letters for each word.

m**o**ney

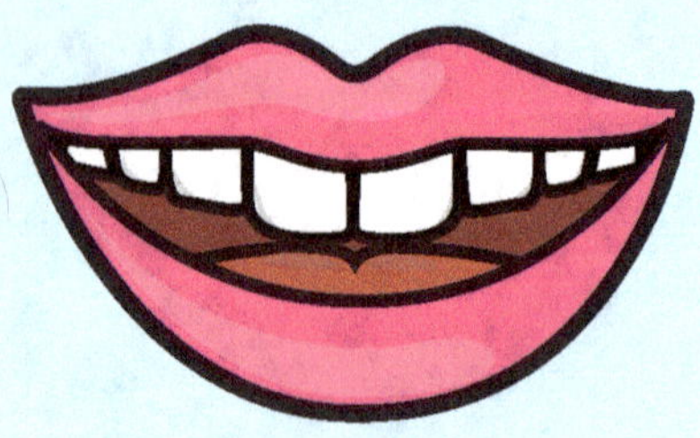

mo**u**th

HERE'S HELP!

u o

Look at each picture and fill in the missing letters for each word.

m**o**nkey

or**a**nge

HERE'S HELP!

a o

Look at each picture and fill in the
missing letters for each word.

<u>o</u>wl

on<u>i</u>on

HERE'S HELP!

o   i

Look at each picture and fill in the
missing letters for each word.

oc_topus

pap_er

HERE'S HELP!

c e

Look at each picture and fill in the missing letters for each word.

p**e**ncil

pa**n**da

HERE'S HELP!

n   e

r<u>a</u>dio

ra<u>i</u>nbow

HERE'S HELP!

Look at each picture and fill in the missing letters for each word.

scho_o_l

s_u_n

HERE'S HELP!

a   o

Look at each picture and fill in the missing letters for each word.

t<u>a</u>ble

tra<u>i</u>n

HERE'S HELP!

a   i

Visit

BABY PROFESSOR
EDUCATION KIDS

www.BabyProfessorBooks.com
to download Free Baby Professor eBooks
and view our catalog of new and exciting
Children's Books